UNDER OUR FEET

PEOPLE

EXPLORING THE CIVILIZATIONS OF HUMANS FROM LONG AGO

BY KIRSTY HOLMES

Gareth Stevens
PUBLISHING

Please visit our website, www.garethstevens.com. For a free color catalog of all our high-quality books, call toll free 1-800-542-2595 or fax 1-877-542-2596.

Cataloging-in-Publication Data

Names: Holmes, Kirsty.
Title: People / Kirsty Holmes.
Description: New York : Gareth Stevens Publishing, 2022. | Series: Under our feet | Includes glossary and index.
Identifiers: ISBN 9781538270493 (pbk.) | ISBN 9781538270516 (library bound) | ISBN 9781538270509 (6 pack) | ISBN 9781538270523 (ebook)
Subjects: LCSH: Fossil hominids--Juvenile literature. | Paleoanthropology--Juvenile literature. | Human remains (Archaeology)--Juvenile literature. | Excavations (Archaeology)--Juvenile literature.
Classification: LCC GN282.H68 2022 | DDC 569.9--dc23

Published in 2022 by
Gareth Stevens Publishing
29 East 21st Street
New York, NY 10010

Copyright © 2022 Booklife Publishing
This edition is published by arrangement with Booklife Publishing

Edited by: Madeline Tyler
Designed by: Dan Scase

Printed in the United States of America

CPSIA compliance information: Batch #BSGS22: For further information contact Gareth Stevens, New York, New York, at 1-800-542-2595.

PHOTO CREDITS

Front Page – Mrkevvzime, komkrit Preechachanwate, BlackMac, Mooi Design, VikiVector, Bragapictures, lacuarela. 4–5 – Masarik, Dima Zel, Daniel Prudek, Twinsterphoto, blvdone, Ryan DeBerardinis. 6–7 – Xolodan, Sergey Kamshylin, Reklamer, The Portable Antiquities Scheme –PAS–, Rebeca Ker Hoshen, Anton-Ivanov, Bork, yingko, Tatsiana Hendzel, Aggie 11. 8–9 – jps, nevio, Leeloona, gerasimov-foto–174, The Portable Antiquities Scheme, Wolfgang Sauber, Roni Setiawan. 10–11 – GregGrabowski, Juan Aunion, Ephraim33, Faviel-Raven. 12–13 – Nick Brundle, Jaroslav Moravcik, Yveke, Harry Burton, Naeblys, Anton Belo. 14–15 – Southern Vadim, Zuktenvos, HelloRF Zcool, Natali Nekrasova, Zde, Bjoertvedt. 16–17 – The Portable Antiquities Scheme, Sven Rosborn, Bullenwachter, Nationalmuseet, Lennart Larsen, Peter Lindberg. 18–19 – Andrey-Kuzmin, GrahamMoore999, Otter, Romaine, antb, Peter Lorimer, Rebecca Rye Photography, Kathryn Sullivan, Simon Annable. 20–21 – Yuan, Zhongyi, pcruciatti, Camphora, Kevin Poh, Hans Wagemaker, Joshua Davenport, DnDavis, Hung Chung Chih, luceluce, Ori Artiste. 22–23 – Romas–Photo, Darryl Brooks, balounm, BlackMac, giannimarchetti, Naaman Abreu, ho visto nina volar. 24–25 – Amitchell125, Harold John Phillips, Gernot Keller, Jononmac46, Geni, British Museum, Michel wal. 26–27 – Keith Michael Taylor, Kristopher Kettner, MarcvanKessel.com, Rainer Lesniewski, Amy Nichole Harris, Amy Nichole Harris. 28–29 – Andreas Praefcke, Jacek Wojnarowski, Nick Atkins, Richard Buckley, Mathew Morris, Jo Appleby, Turi King, Deirdre O–Sullivan, Lin Foxhall, Internet Archive Book Images, RobinLeicester, Richard III of England, Melinda Racz. Background on all pages– komkrit Preechachanwate. Brown Paper throughout – Picsfive. Clipboard throughout – Photo Melon. Bones–skulls throughout – Henri et George, Potapov Alexander, Picsfive. All images courtesty of Shutterstock.com. With thanks to Getty Images, Thinkstock Photo, and iStockphoto.

CONTENTS

Page 4	Under Our Feet
Page 6	Sleeping in the Soil
Page 8	The Stone Age
Page 10	Lucy
Page 12	Tutankhamun
Page 14	The Bronze Age
Page 16	The Iron Age
Page 18	The Romans
Page 20	The Terracotta Army
Page 22	Pompeii
Page 24	Sutton Hoo
Page 26	Rapa Nui
Page 28	The King in the Car Lot
Page 30	People Quiz
Page 31	Glossary
Page 32	Index

Words that look like <u>this</u> are explained in the glossary on page 31.

UNDER OUR FEET

IT'S AWESOME ABOVE YOUR HEAD...

Humans have always looked up at the skies and tried to make sense of what they saw. We have always reached for the stars, climbed to the tops of the tallest mountains, and dreamt of life on other planets. We have built amazing skyscrapers and <u>monuments</u> to the heavens. People live in some of the highest places possible – and now some even live in space!

INTERNATIONAL SPACE STATION

IT'S AMAZING ALL AROUND YOU

There aren't many places you can go on Earth to be truly alone. With over 7 billion people on Earth, we're usually surrounded by people – from our families and the people we live with to densely populated cities that are home to millions of human beings all living out their lives around us.

LOOK DOWN...

Have you ever thought about the people beneath our feet, though? No, we're not talking about today's people, whizzing along in underground trains, or digging and mining just below the surface. We mean the bones, tools, and treasures of people who walked the surface of Earth long ago – and who would have stood and looked at the same stars we do today. These people have kept their secrets for hundreds and even thousands of years, and their stories lie just under our feet!

SLEEPING IN THE SOIL

DID YOU KNOW...?

The art and science of looking for the things ancient people left behind is called archaeology.

Trash heaps may not sound very interesting to us, but ancient ones can teach archaeologists a lot about the past.

THIS BROKEN TOY WAS THROWN AWAY DURING WORLD WAR TWO.

THIS ARCHAEOLOGIST IS CAREFULLY EXCAVATING A SKELETON.

Things that archaeologists find are called artifacts.

Artifacts can tell us a lot about how the people before us lived. This artifact, the Rosetta Stone, was found in Egypt. It shows the same text in three different languages. This meant that Egyptian hieroglyphic writing could be properly translated for the first time.

AKROTIRI, SANTORINI (GREECE), IS AN IMPORTANT SITE FOR ARCHAEOLOGISTS.

There's so much to see
Up here on the street.
But it's even more interesting
Under our feet!

FACT FILE: ARCHAEOLOGY

- Some archaeological sites can be seen from the surface.
- Others are buried beneath the ground.
- Archaeologists must dig carefully – artifacts can be very <u>fragile</u>.
- Archaeologists use tools such as spoons, knives, picks, brushes, and shovels.

THINGS ARCHAEOLOGISTS LOOK FOR

HUMAN REMAINS

BUILDINGS

POSSESSIONS

DIG DEEP

Archaeologists look for any signs of humans they can find. By looking carefully at the artifacts they find, archaeologists can begin to understand how people lived long ago. Bones and bodies can tell us about what people ate, how they lived, and how they died. Their <u>possessions</u> – and how they stored them – can tell us about their <u>technology</u>, beliefs, and culture. And by looking at their buildings, we can learn about their <u>societies</u> and how they all lived together.

THE STONE AGE

Thousands of years ago, people did not have metal and plastic to make things. The people who lived then made their tools from stone, and so we call this time the Stone Age. This was also a time before people wrote anything down, so we call it prehistory. Because people didn't write their stories, everything we know about prehistoric people comes from the artifacts found by archaeologists.

TOOLS

Most animals do not make tools. But we know our ancestors from the Stone Age did because we have found some of their tools! Tools such as ax heads, arrowheads, and knives have all been found, often made from a type of stone called flint. This tells us that our ancestors must have been very smart – it takes skills and knowledge to make and use tools.

STONE AX HEAD, FOUND IN DENMARK

Early Stone Age people used simple tools, like this hand ax. The ax would have been slowly chipped from the stone, in a process called flint knapping.

Later Stone Age axes are polished and smooth. Our ancestors became very good at working stone!

THESE PICKS ARE FROM AROUND 2.6 MILLION TO 11,700 YEARS AGO.

Small arrowheads and <u>serrated</u> harpoons could have been used for fishing. If these are found near a river, this gives us more clues.

HUNTERS

Early humans didn't have sharp teeth, long claws, or great strength like many animals of the time did. Instead, they needed sharp tools to help them survive. We can look at the tiny pieces of stone left over from the Stone Age and have a good idea about what life was like for early people.

THESE HARPOONS FROM THOUSANDS OF YEARS AGO WOULD HAVE BEEN USED TO CATCH SEA CREATURES.

We have found deer bones near <u>settlements</u>, suggesting deer was on the Stone Age menu.

LUCY
3 MILLION YEARS AGO

In 1974, a man named Donald Johanson was on an archaeological dig in Ethiopia, Africa, when he spotted part of a small elbow bone. This bone was part of a larger skeleton that belonged to an ancestor of very early humans! They named this skeleton Lucy.

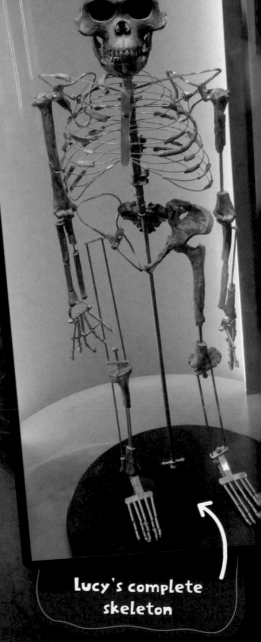

Lucy's complete skeleton

This is what people think Lucy may have looked like when she was alive.

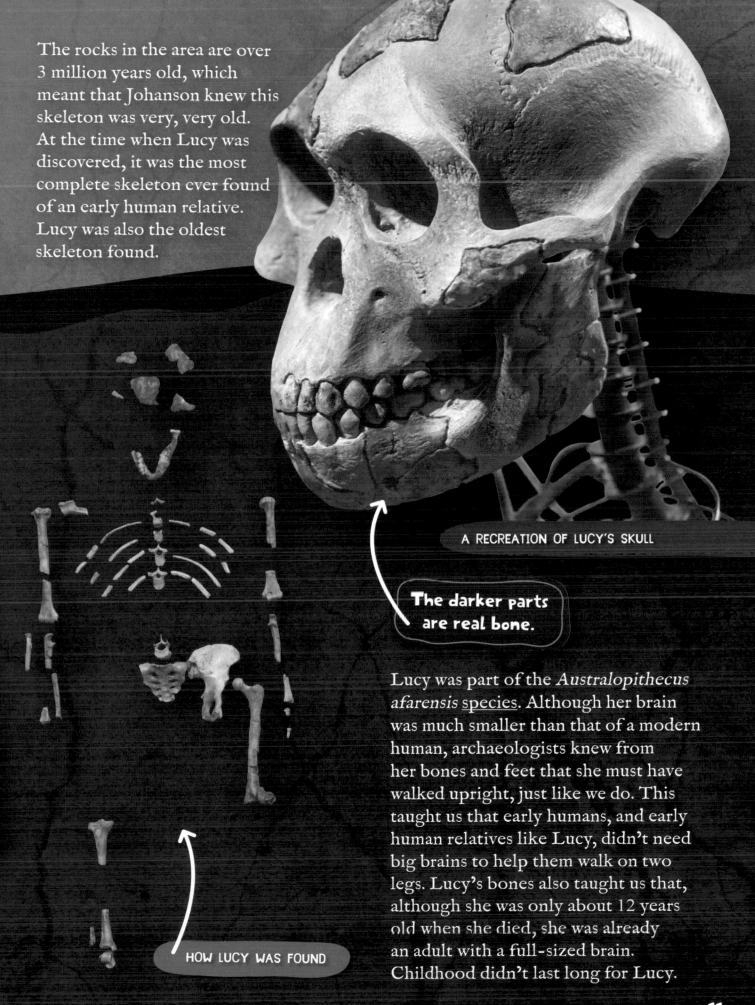

The rocks in the area are over 3 million years old, which meant that Johanson knew this skeleton was very, very old. At the time when Lucy was discovered, it was the most complete skeleton ever found of an early human relative. Lucy was also the oldest skeleton found.

A RECREATION OF LUCY'S SKULL

The darker parts are real bone.

Lucy was part of the *Australopithecus afarensis* species. Although her brain was much smaller than that of a modern human, archaeologists knew from her bones and feet that she must have walked upright, just like we do. This taught us that early humans, and early human relatives like Lucy, didn't need big brains to help them walk on two legs. Lucy's bones also taught us that, although she was only about 12 years old when she died, she was already an adult with a full-sized brain. Childhood didn't last long for Lucy.

HOW LUCY WAS FOUND

TUTANKHAMUN
THE BOY KING OF EGYPT

Between 1333 BC and 1323 BC, a young boy ruled over all of ancient Egypt. His name was Tutankhamun. He was nine years old when he became pharaoh, and just 19 when he died. He was laid to rest in a small tomb. Over time, the tomb was built over and forgotten. That is, until a British archaeologist named Howard Carter peered through the sealed doorway, candle in hand, in 1922...

INTO THE TOMB

As the 3,000-year-old air rushed past him, Carter was able to make out an amazing sight by the flickering light of his candle. Tutankhamun's tomb was right before his eyes. We learned a lot from Carter's amazing find! Because the tomb was surprisingly small for a pharoah, archaeologists think that he must have died suddenly and unexpectedly. Images on the walls of the chamber told us how he was prepared for death and the afterlife, and the treasures themselves told us how rich Tutankhamun's dynasty had been, and how the Egyptians thought death and burial were very important.

"... the interior of the chamber gradually loomed... with its strange and wonderful medley of extraordinary and beautiful objects, heaped upon one another."
~ Howard Carter

The tomb of Tutankhamun lay undisturbed for thousands of years.

This heavy gold death mask was placed over the mummy. A death mask was made to look exactly like the dead person and was placed over their face when they were buried.

This tomb painting shows the Opening of the Mouth ceremony where the mummy's mouth was magically opened so he could eat, drink, and breathe in the afterlife.

THIS THRONE WAS FOUND IN THE TOMB.

THIS WAS A SMALL TOMB FOR A KING. THIS TELLS US THAT PERHAPS THE KING DIED SUDDENLY AND HAD TO USE SOMEONE ELSE'S TOMB IN A HURRY!

HOWARD CARTER IN THE TOMB, 1922

The seal on Tutankhamun's tomb was not broken when Carter found it. He must have looked at this and known that whatever lay behind the door had not been disturbed for thousands of years. What a moment!

THE BRONZE AGE

The Bronze Age of a <u>civilization</u> begins when people start to make their tools from one of the first metals that humans learned to use – bronze. Bronze is an <u>alloy</u> of two metals – tin and copper. The Bronze Age in China began around 3000 BC, but the use of bronze did not reach further west until much later.

A BRONZE AGE SWORD

By working out the ages of objects, we can figure out which ones were used first, and see how they changed as the people got better and better at making them. At first, most Bronze Age civilizations used small amounts of copper to make small or precious objects. We know this because the copper items we find are often older than bronze ones. As they got better at working metal, bronze took over.

DURING THE SHANG DYNASTY (AROUND 1600–1046 BC), THE PEOPLE OF CHINA WERE EXPERT BRONZE WORKERS. BECAUSE WE KNOW THAT THE CHINESE BRONZE AGE STARTED SO MUCH EARLIER THAN EUROPE'S, WE CAN SAFELY IMAGINE THAT THEIR CIVILIZATION WAS MORE ADVANCED.

BRONZE AGE ARTIFACTS ON DISPLAY IN A MUSEUM

BEAKER FOLK

Around 4,500 years ago, a new style of pottery appeared in Spain. The bell-shaped, curved beakers soon spread across Europe and reached Britain. We know this because archaeologists have found these beakers and studied them. Archaeologists can also study the people who were buried with these beakers, known as the Bell-Beaker folk, and learn more about them. The Bell-Beaker folk brought new technology to Britain and introduced the people there to the Bronze Age.

The bell-shaped bottoms of the beakers makes them easy to spot. Archaeologists who find these know they are looking at something that belonged to a Bell-Beaker person thousands of years ago.

BY MAPPING WHERE THE BEAKERS ARE FOUND, AND LOOKING AT THE AGE OF THE BEAKERS, WE CAN CREATE A MAP OF HOW THE BELL-BEAKER FOLK SPREAD ACROSS EUROPE.

By looking at what is buried with the Bell-Beaker folk, archaeologists can find out a lot about the Bell-Beaker folk's culture. These wrist guards, used to protect a soldier's wrist, tell us that the Bell-Beaker folk must have used bows and arrows.

These stone knives and copper daggers were found with the beakers. This tells us that the Bell-Beaker folk were right on the edge of both Stone Age and Bronze Age technology. This helps us figure out when this technology was being used.

THE IRON AGE

The Iron Age follows the Stone Age and the Bronze Age. People were good at working metals now, and iron was stronger than bronze. This meant that new, stronger weapons and farming tools could be made. People began to settle into communities together.

Even though iron is stronger than bronze, there is one downside if you are an archaeologist – iron rusts! This means finds from the Iron Age are rarer than some other types of artifacts.

RUSTED IRON AGE DAGGER

BOG BODIES

It's not just weapons and tools that interest archaeologists. Human bodies are a grisly but important find for a historian. This is a chance to come face-to-face – literally – with our ancestors, after all!

OSTERBY MAN WAS FOUND IN GERMANY WITH HIS HAIRSTYLE PERFECTLY PRESERVED.

THIS IS TOLLUND MAN, FOUND IN DENMARK IN 1950.

Hundreds of bodies, most of them from the Iron Age, have been found in the wetlands of Northern Europe. The oldest of these bodies is 10,000 years old! Because they have been buried in the wet, thick mud, the bodies are often amazingly well preserved. Some have been found with fingerprints, hair, and fingernails!

This is the bog body known as **Grauballe Man**, discovered in **Denmark**. His <u>facial expression</u> is preserved perfectly — even the lines on his face.

This is the 2,000-year-old clothing found on the bog body known as the **Wife of Huldremose**. She was found wearing this cloak and checked skirt. The waters have turned her clothes brown, but archaeologists were able to discover that her skirt was blue, and her scarf was red.

We do not know why these bodies ended up in the bogs. There are lots of theories. Some think they could have been part of a grisly religious ceremony – or perhaps they were <u>deserters</u> from the army who had been executed? Archaeologists can look at each body in great detail and find out a lot about how they lived – and maybe even how they died...

THIS IS THE BOCKSTEN BOG MAN, FOUND IN SWEDEN. HE WAS WEARING A CLOAK WHEN HE DIED, AND FELL TO THE BOTTOM OF A LAKE WHICH LATER BECAME A BOG.

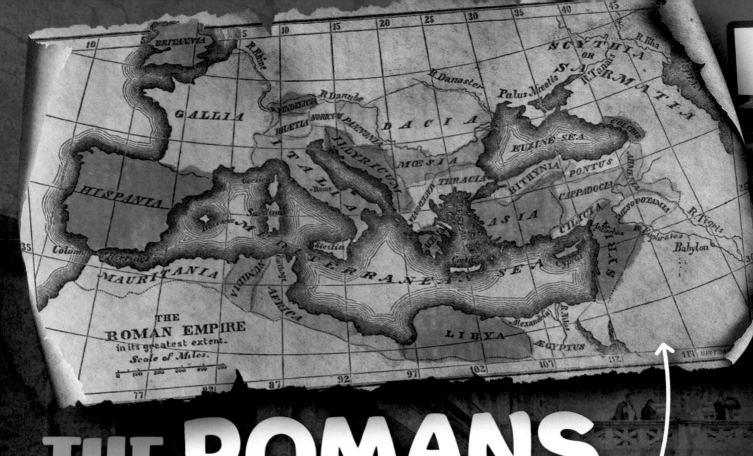

THE **ROMANS**

At its largest, the Roman Empire covered huge areas of what we now call Europe, Asia, and Africa. Archaeologists who are interested in the ancient Romans are lucky – we have writings, stories, and pictures from ancient Rome that tell us a lot about the people who lived then.

The ancient Romans took their culture wherever they went, and we can see it in the artifacts that are found across their old empire, from Britain to the Middle East. By looking at these artifacts, we can understand more about how the ancient Romans changed the lives and futures of the people they ruled.

THIS ROMAN LATRINE AT HOUSESTEADS ROMAN FORT ON HADRIAN'S WALL IN THE UK SHOWS HOW ROMAN PLUMBING AND SANITATION HAD SPREAD TO THE UK.

A ROMAN TEMPLE ONCE STOOD HERE IN CAERWENT, WALES...

... AND HERE IN TAWERN, GERMANY.

Can you see the similarities?

ROMAN BATHS WERE AN IMPORTANT PLACE TO BATHE AND MEET UP WITH PEOPLE. THIS MIGHT LOOK LIKE IT BELONGS IN ROME, BUT IT'S ACTUALLY A PHOTO FROM A TOWN CALLED BATH IN THE UK!

THE ROMANS INTRODUCED WRITING TO BRITAIN. THEY WERE GREAT RECORD KEEPERS AND LEFT A LOT OF INFORMATION ABOUT LIFE IN ROMAN BRITAIN.

Roman roads are famous for being wide and very straight. They can be seen all over Europe and in parts of Asia.

SARDINIA

JORDAN

ENGLAND

THE TERRACOTTA ARMY

STANDING GUARD IN THE SOIL

Near Lishan in the Shaanxi Province in China, the first emperor of China was laid to rest in a grand <u>mausoleum</u>. The year was 210 BC, and his name was Qin Shi Huangdi. We know that the emperor wanted to live forever. He sent people out in search of special potions that would allow him to live forever. Although he did die in the end, he will be remembered for a long time thanks to his Terracotta Army.

In AD 1974, two farmers were digging when they struck something solid. To their surprise, they had found a life-sized clay soldier, ready for battle. The mausoleum of Qin Shi Huangdi had been discovered again, and nobody was expecting what they found. Archaeologists carefully excavated 8,000 terracotta soldiers who had stood for over 2,000 years, guarding the tomb of the first emperor of China. Each figure was unique, and that wasn't all. The amazing detail on the soldiers, horses, chariots, weapons, and other items found in the pits gave archaeologists an incredible record of what ancient Chinese people looked like when they went to war, and the kinds of weapons they may have used.

EACH SOLDIER'S FACE IS UNIQUE. IT IS ESTIMATED THERE MAY BE UP TO 8,000 SOLDIERS IN TOTAL.

QIN SHI HUANGDI WILL BE REMEMBERED FOREVER.

HORSES, CHARIOTS, AND WAGONS WERE ALL LEFT TO TAKE THE EMPEROR INTO THE AFTERLIFE IN STYLE.

THE SOLDIERS WOULD ORIGINALLY HAVE BEEN PAINTED BRIGHTLY, BUT OVER TIME THE PAINT HAS WORN AWAY. CAN YOU SPOT THE SOLDIER'S BRIGHT GOLDEN SCARF?

ARCHAEOLOGISTS WORKING ON THE EXCAVATION

IT IS ESTIMATED THAT QIN SHI HUANGDI ORDERED WORK ON THE MAUSOLEUM TO BEGIN SHORTLY AFTER BECOMING EMPEROR. HUNDREDS OF THOUSANDS OF WORKERS MIGHT HAVE WORKED ON THE AMAZING MONUMENT.

The tomb of Qin Shi Huangdi remains undisturbed. It is said that traps were sct to stop anyone from robbing the grave, and that amazing treasures fill the tomb.

POMPEII A LOST CITY

Overlooking the Bay of Naples in Italy stands Mount Vesuvius, a powerful volcano. It has erupted over 50 times. In AD 79, an eruption buried the nearby city of Pompeii, covering both the buildings and people in a thick layer of powdery volcanic ash. The city was abandoned and forgotten...

POMPEII AND MOUNT VESUVIUS

In AD 1775, the city was rediscovered under just a few feet of volcanic material, where it had been lying for almost 2,000 years. The entire city had been frozen in time, perfectly preserved in fine volcanic ash. By the 1990s, most of the city had been revealed, and an incredible amount of information had been discovered. Archaeologists were able to walk the streets, read the graffiti on the walls, and even stand face-to-face with the people who perished in Pompeii that day...

THE PEOPLE OF POMPEII

One of the most unique and remarkable finds in Pompeii were the people themselves. When the huge cloud of hot gas hanging over the volcano collapsed, sending wave after wave of super-hot ash and air, it killed everything and everyone in its path. The fine stone that rained down formed a shell around the people and animals where they lay. As the bodies slowly broke down, a space was left. When archaeologists filled these holes with plaster, then chipped away the ash around them, they were amazed to see how well the ash had frozen these people in time, the agony of their final moments clear on their faces...

THIS MAN LOOKS LIKE HE WAS TRYING TO CLIMB TO SAFETY.

A BOY HIDES HIS FACE.

THESE PEOPLE MUST HAVE GROUPED TOGETHER AS THE VOLCANO ERUPTED. COULD THEY HAVE BEEN A FAMILY?

THE STREETS OF POMPEII

The volcanic ash also preserved the streets, buildings, and artifacts of Pompeii. This gave us an amazing look at life in this city. Villas, fountains, homes, and public places were all hidden under the ashes, and we can even see the remains of the animals that lived alongside the people there.

THIS ANCIENT GRAFFITI WAS FOUND ON A WALL IN POMPEII.

THESE SKELETONS OF HORSES SHOW US THIS MUST HAVE BEEN A STABLE.

WE CAN SEE THE COLORS ON THE WALLS ARE STILL VIBRANT AND CLEAR.

THE HOUSE OF THE FAUN

Pompeii's richest house is known as the House of the Faun. Many amazing treasures have been found here, including some beautiful mosaics. Mosaics are a type of art made by putting lots of small tiles together to form a larger pattern or picture. This mosaic of Alexander the Great was found at the House of the Faun.

SUTTON HOO

Edith Pretty was a wealthy woman who lived in a grand house called Sutton Hoo House in Suffolk, England. After her husband died, she began to wonder about the strange, grassy mounds that dotted her estate. She decided they could not be natural and thought they must be worth excavating, so she sought the help of a local man, Basil Brown. Basil knew about rocks and archaeology as he had taught himself, and together they began to dig up one of the most interesting back gardens ever!

THE BURIAL MOUNDS AT SUTTON HOO

THE GHOSTLY IMAGE OF A SHIP CAN BE SEEN PRESSED INTO THE MOUND. THE SHIP ROTTED AWAY LONG AGO, BUT YOU CAN STILL SEE THE MARKS AND PATTERNS THAT IT LEFT BEHIND.

Historians were able to reconstruct the burial chamber thanks to Edith's curiosity and Basil's careful work. It may have looked like this. Many of the metal objects remained after the body disappeared.

When Basil found an iron <u>rivet</u>, he recognized it as belonging to an ancient ship. But what would a ship be doing in the grounds of a grand house? Basil and Edith knew they were looking at the site of an ancient burial — and only very important people were given the honor of a ship burial.

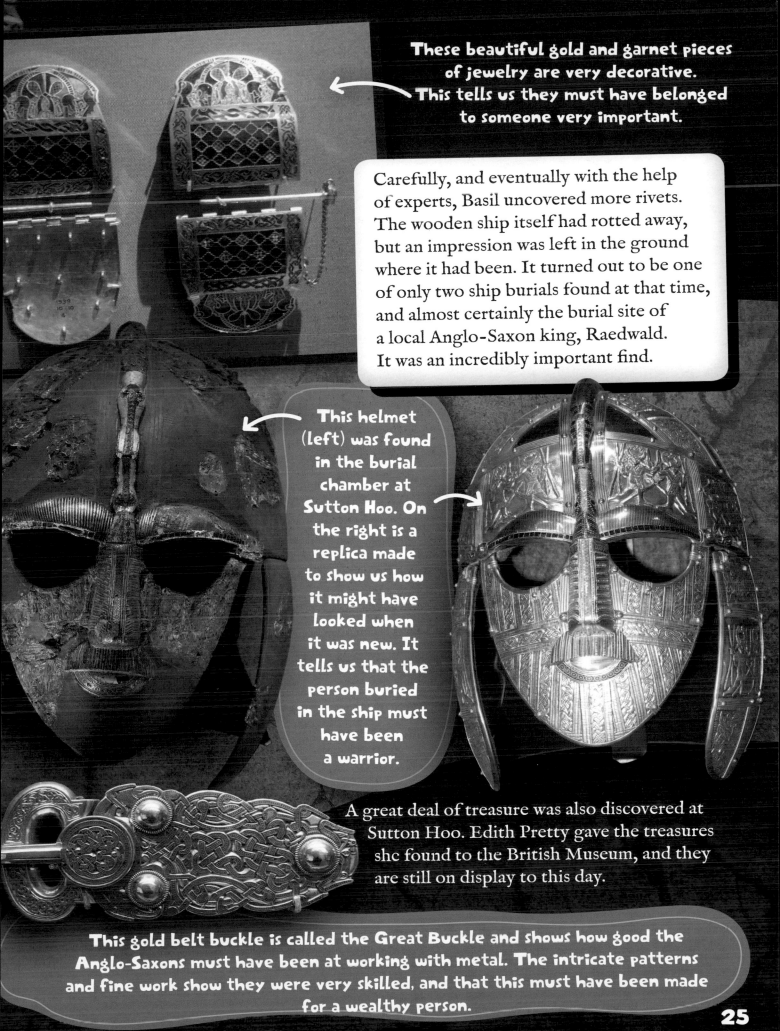

These beautiful gold and garnet pieces of jewelry are very decorative. This tells us they must have belonged to someone very important.

Carefully, and eventually with the help of experts, Basil uncovered more rivets. The wooden ship itself had rotted away, but an impression was left in the ground where it had been. It turned out to be one of only two ship burials found at that time, and almost certainly the burial site of a local Anglo-Saxon king, Raedwald. It was an incredibly important find.

This helmet (left) was found in the burial chamber at Sutton Hoo. On the right is a replica made to show us how it might have looked when it was new. It tells us that the person buried in the ship must have been a warrior.

A great deal of treasure was also discovered at Sutton Hoo. Edith Pretty gave the treasures she found to the British Museum, and they are still on display to this day.

This gold belt buckle is called the Great Buckle and shows how good the Anglo-Saxons must have been at working with metal. The intricate patterns and fine work show they were very skilled, and that this must have been made for a wealthy person.

RAPA NUI

Out in the Pacific Ocean lies the island of Rapa Nui. Rapa Nui is one of the world's most isolated places, and it is over 1,000 miles (1,600 km) to the nearest island. However, if you stood on the shores of Rapa Nui, you probably wouldn't feel alone. Scattered across the island are 887 huge statues, made by early Rapa Nui people. They are the moai.

THE MYSTERIOUS AND PROUD FACES CAN BE FOUND ALL OVER THE ISLAND.

A GROUP OF MOAI STANDING ON AN AHU

The enormous monuments were at first thought to be only heads, as they had slowly become buried in the soil over time, but we now know these sleeping giants have torsos too, and some are kneeling figures. Almost all of them have enormous heads – almost three-fifths of their total height is head! Many have been placed on ahu – large stone platforms. But what are they – and why were they built?

Jacob Roggeveen was the first European person to visit the island when he landed there in 1722. He called it Easter Island because he landed there on Easter Sunday.

SOME MOAI HAVE THEIR EYES PAINTED ON, AND WEAR THESE LARGE HATS.

Most moai were carved from volcanic rock. They were carved by hand and may have taken five to six people around a year to finish. Only about one-quarter of them made it to their final resting places, looking over the island of Rapa Nui and out to sea. One of the largest that has been found is known as Paro. Paro weighs 82 tons (74 tonnes), and is 32 feet (9.8 m) tall. For a long time, people weren't sure what the moai were for, but it's now believed that each statue represents the <u>ancestral</u> head of a family.

Today, around 5,800 people live on Rapa Nui, and many of them are related to the people who carved these mysterious faces.

SOME MOAI WERE TOPPLED AND STILL LAY IN THE SOIL.

THE KING IN THE CAR LOT

There are a lot of stories about King Richard III of England – and not all of them are true. But perhaps the most amazing is the story of how his remains were found, right under our feet...

Richard III was born in 1452, became king in 1483, and died in 1485 at the Battle of Bosworth in England. The Battle of Bosworth was won by Henry Tudor, who became King Henry VII. After the battle, the Tudors went to a lot of effort to make sure that everyone knew how Richard III was a terrible and villainous king. Even the famous playwright William Shakespeare wrote a play, showing Richard plotting to kill children and doing all sorts of terrible things, making him seem even more awful. But was this true?

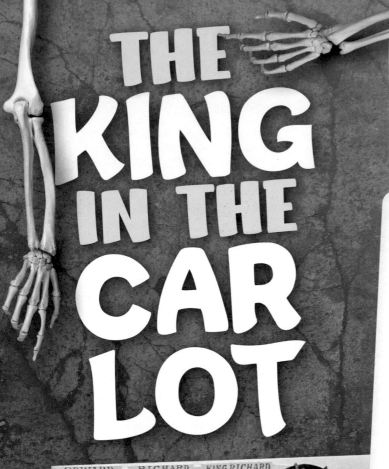

In the play, Richard is shown to have a limp and a withered arm. Henry is shown as tall, strong, and heroic. Could the Tudors have wanted to show Richard as evil to make themselves look better? After all, they were paying Shakespeare for the play...

KING RICHARD III NOW LIES IN LEICESTER CATHEDRAL.

RICHARD III

Loyaulte me lie

After the battle, a group of holy men called the Grey Friars took the king's body and buried him in the grounds of their church. Over time, the church was demolished, buried, and forgotten. Many years later, archaeologists thought they had figured out where the church had been – but there was one problem. There was now a parking lot there! They carefully began to excavate the area, and sure enough found the church. And, most amazingly, at the north end of the lot they found a skeleton of a man with battle wounds and a curved spine...

THIS IS HOW KING RICHARD III MIGHT HAVE LOOKED. IT'S MUCH MORE ACCURATE NOW THAT WE HAVE HIS REMAINS.

Shakespeare described Richard III's curved spine in his play, and now historians had proof that it wasn't made up. By looking at his skull, historians could see exactly how he died, and by looking at his remains they could even tell what he ate.

RICHARD III'S SIGNATURE

What a day it must've been for the archaeologists when the face of the king in the parking lot saw daylight again. What an exciting find!

Imagine how many people must have walked across this car lot, with no idea that one of the most infamous kings of England lay under their feet...

29

PEOPLE QUIZ

QUESTIONS

1. Which language could finally be translated thanks to the Rosetta Stone?
2. What is the process of shaping flint to make tools called?
3. How do we know Lucy walked upright?
4. What was Pharaoh Tutankhamun's death mask made of?
5. Which two metals make bronze?
6. What color was the skirt the Wife of Huldremose was wearing?
7. What year was Emperor Qin Shi Huangdi buried in his mausoleum?
8. What was the name of the volcano that buried Pompeii?
9. What did Edith Pretty and Basil Brown find at Sutton Hoo?
10. How many moai are there on Rapa Nui?
11. What is the name of one of the largest moai?
12. Who wrote a play about King Richard III?
13. Where was King Richard III finally found?

ANSWERS

1. Egyptian hieroglyphs.
2. Flint knapping.
3. From her bones and feet.
4. Gold.
5. Tin and copper.
6. Blue.
7. 210 BC.
8. Vesuvius.
9. An ancient ship burial.
10. 887.
11. Paro.
12. Shakespeare.
13. Under a car lot.

GLOSSARY

afterlife – a religious belief that there is another life after death

alloy – a mixture of two or more metals

ancestors – people from whom one is descended, for example a great-grandparent

ancestral – having to do with ancestors

civilization – the society, culture, and way of life of a certain area

deserters – people who run away in a war

dynasty – a period of time that is ruled by a series of people from the same family

excavating – carefully removing bits of earth from an area in order to uncover buried remains or ruins

facial expression – when the face is used to show emotions or thoughts, such as smiles or frowns

fragile – easily broken

infamous – well known for being bad or evil

isolated – separated and alone

latrine – a toilet

mausoleum – a large elaborate tomb, or a building that holds a tomb

monuments – buildings or structures built to remember someone or something

pharaoh – a ruler in ancient Egypt

possessions – physical things that someone owns

preserved – kept in its original form

remains – parts that have been left behind; usually referring to a dead body

rivet – a metal bolt that holds plates of metal together

rusts – when iron turns reddish-brown

sanitation – to do with making things clean and not dangerous to health

serrated – to have small notches or teeth like a saw that help to cut

settlements – places where people choose to live and build communities

societies – collections of people living together

species – a group of very similar animals or plants that are capable of producing young together

technology – devices or tools to help us do something

torsos – the parts of bodies from the neck to the hips

INDEX

A

ahu 26
archaeologists 6–8, 11–12,
        15–18, 20–22, 29
archaeology 6–7, 10, 24
arrows 8–9, 15
artifacts 6–8, 14, 16, 18, 23
Australopithecus afarensis
        11
ax heads 8

B

Bath 19
Bell-Beaker folk 15
bog bodies 16–17
bones 5, 7, 9–11
Britain 14–15, 18–19
bronze 14–16
Brown, Basil 24–25

C

Carter, Howard 12–13
China 14, 20

E

Egypt 6, 12
Ethiopia 10

G

graffiti 22–23

H

House of the Faun 23

J

Johanson, Donald 10–11

K

King Raedwald 25

L

Leicester 28

M

moai 26–27

P

Paro 27
pharaohs 12
prehistory 8
Pretty, Edith 24–25

Q

Qin Shi Huangdi 20–21

R

Rapa Nui 26–27
Richard III 28–29
Roggeveen, Jacob 26
Roman baths 19
Roman Empire 18

S

Shakespeare, William 28–29
Shang Dynasty 14
society 7
soldiers 15, 20–21

T

tombs 12–13, 20–21
tools 5, 7–9, 14, 16
traps 21
Tudors 28

V

Vesuvius 22